SHANGO
and the
AMAZING Magical
SLEEPING
Spell

Simon Menzies

ISBN-13: 978-1539988618
ISBN- 10: 1539988619

Books in the Shango Series:

- **Sleep** – Shango and the Amazing Magical Sleeping Spell

- **Anxiety** - Shango and the Amazing Magical No Worries Spell

- **Anger** - Shango and the Amazing Magical Calming Spell

- **Fear and Phobias** - Shango and the Amazing Magical Bravery Spell

- **Confidence** - Shango and the Amazing Magical Confidence Spell

PLEASE READ CAREFULLY BEFORE USING THIS PRODUCT

This product may cause drowsiness or sleep in the reader or unintended listeners.

Do not listen to this book while driving or operating machinery. Do not read this book within hearing of someone driving or operating machinery. When reading or listening to this book, choose an environment that is quiet and safe.

Results will vary, each individual will respond differently. We do not claim that there are typical results that all consumers will generally achieve. A small percentage of listeners might be impervious to suggestion and some will accept suggestion faster than others. There are no guarantees that reading or listening to this product will help or resolve specific issues. We take no responsibility for how the listener will respond.

This product is not intended to replace medical treatment. Consult with your Doctor/Physician on all medical issues regarding your child's condition and treatment. The content is not intended to be a substitute for professional medical advice, diagnosis, or treatment. It is not a substitute for a medical examination, nor does it replace the need for services provided by medical professionals. Always seek the advice of your medical professional before making any changes to treatment.

For best results, please follow the Advice and Instructions to Reader. If you encounter problems, the Audio version will provide a controlled rendition of the story and might be more effective. The more the story is repeated, the more effective it will be.

The child must be able to understand the vocabulary used in the story.

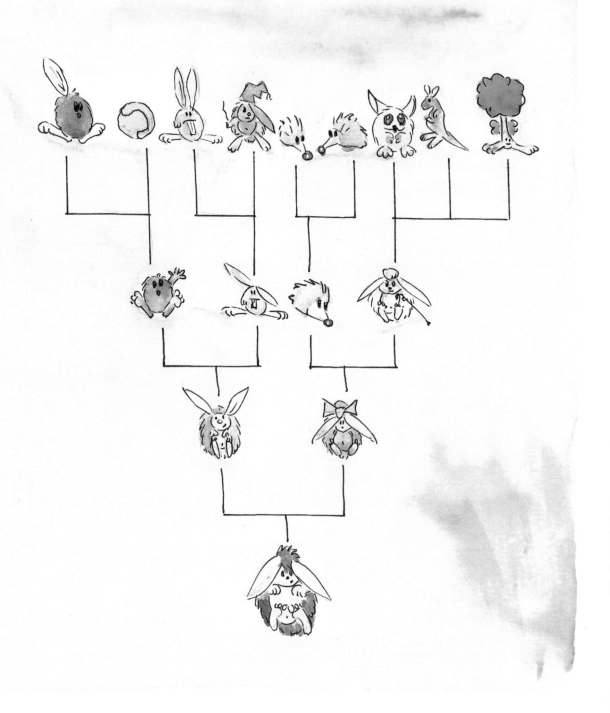

Shango's Family Tree

Advice and Instructions to Reader

If a child consistently has difficulty getting to sleep, this could be due to a passing phase, dietary or psychological issues. In the latter, anxiety or depression might be a cause and if so please see Shango's other books relating to those issues.

Shango hopes to help your child sleep with his magic spell, but if the condition persists and you are concerned, medical or professional advice should be sought.

To improve fluency, please read through the story before reading it to the child.

Use a slow, gentle, rhythmic voice. It may sound silly, but it works.

Emphasize the words in **bold**, with a slow and deliberate tone.

Ensure the child is comfortably in bed and ready to listen before starting.

For the first few times, complete the story EVEN if the child falls asleep before the ending. They will still be able to hear you.

Follow the instructions in bracketed sections [_____], for example [YAWN].

On the last page of the book you will have two options to end on: one is to continue sleeping, the other to continue napping (daytime).

The story uses Positive Suggestion and Repetition to influence the child. It may read oddly, but the language is intentional.

Much of the effectiveness of this book depends on a positive connection between child and reader as well as the reading technique explained above. Some may find the CD/Audio version more effective.

After the first reading of the book, the following day or after waking up, please encourage the child to create their own illustrations of their Shango and Dream World. This is a part of the process of connecting the child to the story and will make the story even more effective on following nights.

Please persevere - The more often the story is read, the more effective it will be.

SHANGO and the Amazing Magical SLEEPING Spell

Shango is a funny little thing and sometimes not. He is bigger than a ladybug and smaller than an elephant and sometimes not. Shango is about the same age as you, perhaps a 100 years older or a 100 years younger, or perhaps not.

Shango is a Tidbog and Tidbogs are relatives of tree-wongles, hedgehogs, bunnies, hamsters, monkeybugs, fizzbogs and a whole bunch of other things.

Shango is a **very sleepy** Tidbog. He was not always **sleepy** like he is now. He did not **sleep well** until he was given the **Amazing Magical Sleeping Spell** of the Tidbog wizards, known as the Wizbogs. But more about that later.....

When Tidbogs are awake they live in our imaginations, but when they **go to sleep** they live in a magical **Dream World**.

Tidbogs can take on many different shapes when they are **asleep**, but when awake they are fluffy and round and sometimes not, with two big eyes, sometimes three, and two big ears, sometimes one, and they can see and hear everything.

Shango lives in a place called Windybottom, so called because it's at the bottom of a windy valley, so they say.

There are lots of Tidbogs, like the Pongalot Tidbogs of Cowpat fields, where you can pat the cows in the fields, so they say. Shango's family are called the Tootberry Tidbogs and for now we are only interested in them and especially in Shango.

No-one knows why the Pongalot Tidbogs pong a lot, **BUT** the Tootberry Tidbogs earned their name because they like to eat tootberries, which are made of bath bubbles and magic and something else. Tootberries make **you feel very, very sleepy** and some scientists think are the cause of the high winds in Windybottom, so they say.

Tidbogs like to live underground in a magical place where they can **sleep safely** and have **dreaming adventures**. Many **sleeps** ago they used to live in trees. The **gentle whooshing of the leaves** in the wind made them **very, very sleepy** [Yawn].

But the wind in Windybottom sometimes would blow them far away and they would often wake up stuck to sheep or woolly socks. This was a big problem for the sheep that liked to wear woolly socks and one of the reasons you do not see sheep in socks anymore apart from in a far off place called the Silly Isles where some still do.

Sheep in Woolly Socks happily going about their business on the Silly Isles.

Once the wind was so strong in Windybottom, Granny Gangapants Tidbog, who is a **very, very sleepy** Tidbog, was blown far away to Africa and stuck to a small elephant's ear. You can imagine the shock when she came out of her **deep, deep sleep**. It was a long walk back of quite a few minutes and when she finally got home she was **very, very tired and sleepy**. Granny Gangapants then went straight **to bed** and fell **into a deep, deep sleep**. [Yawn.]

Tidbogs spend most of their very long lives either **feeling very, very sleepy** or actually being **asleep**.

When Tidbogs **go to sleep**, they travel to the magical **Dream World** where anything can happen, whatever **you** want. They can change shape and colour and **even** be invisible. They can play and **be happy** or just **sleep deeply**. This is why they love to **go to sleep**. [YAWN.]

Granny Gangapants in Africa.

Tidbogs especially love to go to the **Dream World** with their **special friends**, children like **you**. It's the **dream** of every young Tidbog to find their own **special friend** to have adventures with when they **go to sleep**.

Being a young Tidbog, Shango has not found his **special friend**, until now. He **loves you** and he wants **you to be his special friend**. Best friends forever.

Very good.

Shango is feeling **very, very sleepy now**. He wants **to go to sleep** and share with you **the Amazing Magical Sleeping Spell**.

Shango is feeling very **tired now. You are** also feeling much more **sleepy**.

Very sleepy Shango will help you **sleep**. He is **magical** and wants you to come with him into his **Dream World**.

Like you, **sleepy** Shango is very **special**. Even if you just keep your eyes closed and pretend to **be asleep**, you will start on a **magical** journey into your imagination and **you** will **feel more and more sleepy**.

Can you find Shango?

Now for the magic bit:

Shango says you have to blink your eyes three times [CHILD TO BLINK 3 TIMES], now **keep your eyes closed** and whisper very slowly and quietly the Tidbog magic word **FIZZBALLS** [CHILD TO SAY 'FIZZBALLS'] and your magical journey will begin.

Very good.

Shango wants you to keep your eyes closed, **do not worry about anything** and just concentrate on my voice. [YAWN.]

Shango says you have to breathe in deeply and when you breathe out slowly, you will notice your **whole body relaxing** and starting to **feel very tired and sleepy**.

[VISIBLY/AUDIBLY BREATHE IN DEEPLY AND THEN SLOWLY OUT IN TIME WITH THE CHILD.]

Well done, that is perfect. Keep breathing in deeply and as you breathe out, your whole body gets **more and more sleepy**. Very good.

Let your **whole body relax** more and more with each breath and just think about Shango and my voice.

You now feel very sleepy and you want to go with Shango to the **Dream World**. You are doing very well.

[KEEP BREATHING DEEPLY AND ENCOURAGING THE CHILD TO RELAX UNTIL YOU FEEL IT APPROPRIATE TO MOVE ON.]

Shango now wants you to see or imagine 10 steps in front of you going down to the **Dream World**. Well done. In a moment, Shango wants you to follow him down the steps. And when **you go down deeper and deeper,** you will hear me count each step from 10 all the way down to 1, and **you will go all the way down** into Shango's **Dream World** where **you will feel safe and happy.** [YAWN] Well done.

[COUNT DOWN SLOWLY WITH A PAUSE BETWEEN NUMBERS, GETTING QUIETER WITH EACH NUMBER.]

Now you see or imagine the steps in front of you, I will start to count you down them, one by one:

10 - you are going down the steps

9 - you are feeling very sleepy

8 - down deeper and deeper to the Dream World

7 - deeper to sleep

6 - sleepier and sleepier

5 - keep going down

4 - down, down to the Dream World

3 - deeper to sleep

2 - you are now very sleepy

1 - you now feel completely asleep.

Well done. You have entered Shango's **Dream World** and soon you can **go on a magical adventure** with Shango.

Shango says just listen to my voice and **do not worry** about any other noises or thoughts. Any familiar noises and every word I say will just help you **go to sleep** more and more.

Shango knows you have a **wonderful imagination** like him. In Shango's magical **Dream World** everything you imagine is real, but **only good and happy** things.

Shango now wants you to imagine a wonderful place where **you feel very happy and safe**. It can be a memory or somewhere real or a new special place you have invented. It is up to you.

Nod your head when you are in your special place where **you feel happy and safe**. [WAIT FOR THE CHILD TO NOD.]

What colour is your Dream World Shango?

Shango now wants you to notice when you think about the **wonderful place you are now in** that the **happy feeling you now have inside you** gets **bigger and bigger**. The more you think about the **happy feeling** the **happier and happier** you feel.

Shango wants you to know now that whenever you think of Shango or hear his name, even when you are awake, this wonderful happy feeling will come back to you, even bigger than it is now.

If you think of Shango's name now you will notice the feeling of **happiness** gets **bigger and bigger** inside yo**u**.

You are doing so well and this makes Shango **very happy**. Shango **loves** you and he knows you **love** him.

In a moment you can go on a wonderful journey with Shango, into the **Dream World**, where **you feel very happy and loved**. Shango will always be with you and help you.

This Wizbog wants to see your Dream World.

Night-time Story Ending

After your adventure with Shango, you will **sleep** very well and you will wake up normally and easily in the morning feeling very happy and loved.

Y**ou know** Shango is now with you always and whenever you think of Shango he will make you feel very **happy** and **loved**.

Next time, when you go down Shango's 10 steps to the **Dream World you will go to sleep very easily and quickly** and 10 times **sleepier** than you are now.

You will **always love** hearing Shango's story and you will look forward to going on more **wonderful** adventures with Shango in the **Dream World**.

If you hear me leaving the room or any other familiar noises, they will just help you **sleep more**.

You just want to **sleep** now and have a **wonderful** adventure with Shango **until the morning** when you will wake up **feeling happy and loved**.

Sleep now…...

Shango loves you. Please draw him something?

Daytime Nap Story Ending

You want to sleep now and have a wonderful **dreaming** adventure with Shango, **you will sleep very well** and when you hear familiar noises around you, **you will go to sleep more and more into the Dream World.**

You will **always love** hearing Shango's story and will look forward to going on more **wonderful** adventures with him in the **Dream World.**

Next time, when you go down Shango's 10 steps to the **Dream World you will go to sleep very quickly and easily** and 10 times **deeper** than you are now.

You will look forward to bedtime and going down to Shango's Dream World again.

After you have had a **good sleep**, you will wake up when your name is spoken and **you will** feel **very happy** and **loved**, but now **you just want to sleep** and have a **lovely dream** time with Shango.

Well done. Sleep now.

[WHEN NAP TIME IS OVER, YOU CAN WAKE THE CHILD UP BY SAYING THE CHILD'S NAME CLEARLY AND FIRMLY. ALLOW THE CHILD A FEW MINUTES TO WAKE UP FULLY.]

Sheep in Socks thinks you are amazing. Can you draw it something?

Can you draw this Fizzbog some magic stuff?

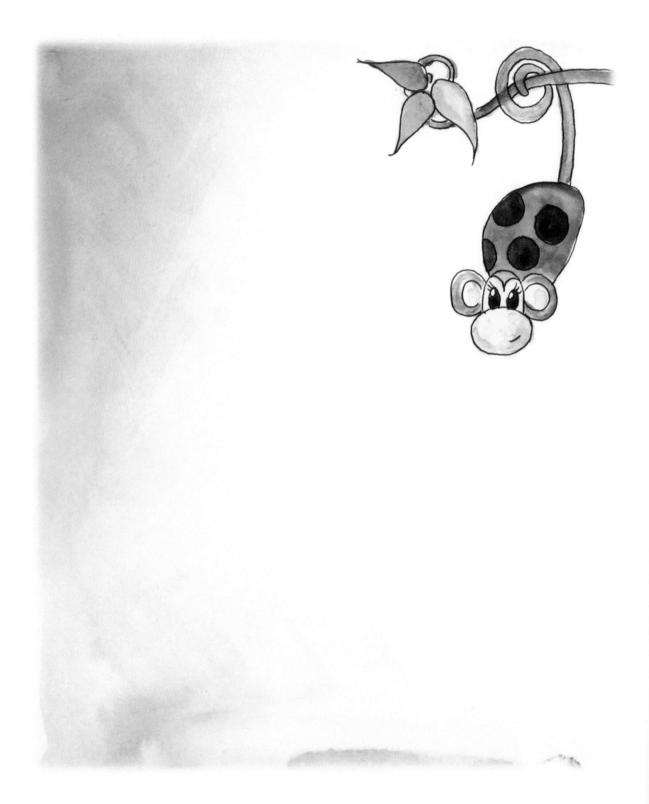

Please draw one of your dream friends for Monkeybug?

Can you draw Pongalot Tidbog your dreams?

Can you draw Bunny something?

Show happy Shango what's in your dreams.

This Thingymajig wants you to draw him a friend.

Printed in Great Britain
by Amazon